D1712428

BILLIE JEAN KING VS. BOBBY RIGGS

Published in the United States of America by Cherry Lake Publishing
Ann Arbor, Michigan
www.cherrylakepublishing.com

Reading Adviser: Marla Conn MS, Ed., Literacy specialist, Read-Ability, Inc.

Photo Credits: ©Mirrorpix/Newscom, cover; ©Mirrorpix/Newscom, 1; ©State Library of Queensland/Wikimedia, 5; ©Keystone Pictures USA/ZUMAPRESS/Newscom, 6; ©Keystone Pictures USA/ZUMAPRESS/Newscom, 9; ©Adrian Murrell/Getty Images, 10; ©Corbis/Splash News/Newscom, 13; ©Corbis/Splash News/Newscom, 14; ©AllsportUK/Getty Images, 15; ©AllsportUK/Getty Images, 19; ©Corbis/Splash News/Newscom, 20; ©Lynn Gilbert/Wikimedia, 21; ©Women's Sports Foundation/Getty Images, 25; ©The Straits Times/Newscom, 26; ©AllsportUK/Getty Images, 28; ©Everett Collection/Newscom, 28; ©Corbis/Splash News/Newscom, 29; ©Tony Duffy/Getty Images, 29; ©Corbis/Splash News/Newscom, 30

Library of Congress Cataloging-in-Publication Data has been filed and is available at catalog.loc.gov

Cherry Lake Publishing would like to acknowledge the work of The Partnership for 21st Century Learning.
Please visit *www.p21.org* for more information.

Printed in the United States of America
Corporate Graphics

ABOUT THE AUTHOR

J.E. Skinner received a Bachelor of Arts in Anthropology from Wake Forest University. She loves writing both fiction and nonfiction books. In addition to reading as much as she can, when J.E. isn't writing, she is hiking with her dogs and spending time with her family in the beautiful outdoors.

TABLE OF CONTENTS

CHAPTER 1

The Game That Started a Movement

Tennis is played on either a hard, grass, or clay court. The game originated in France between the 11th and 13th centuries, and was called *jeu de paume*, meaning "game of the palm." The word "tennis" derives from *tenez*, which translates loosely to "here it comes." Players would shout this phrase as they were about to serve.

By the 1860s, tennis had become more popular than croquet. In the mid-1870s, tennis was given a set of rules that is still followed today. Scores start at "love," or zero, and increase to 15, 30, 40, and "game." There are six games per set, and 3 to 5 sets per match.

An early game of tennis, circa 1890.

Interest surged around 1968, when tennis turned professional. The addition of several Open tournaments increased enthusiasm and provided a faster level of play. The use of brightly colored clothing added extra excitement.

Today, about 18 million people play tennis annually. Tournaments, camps, and clubs allow players of all skill levels to practice and hone their abilities. Almost 1,200 universities sponsor nearly 11,000 students for their varsity teams each year. Tennis started as a simple distraction and became a dominant global sport participated in and watched worldwide.

Americans hold a winning trophy from the 1964 match at Wimbledon.

One of the most famous matches ever played was between Billie Jean King and Bobby Riggs. They were two of the best tennis players in the entire sport. The match took place in 1973 and was called the "Battle of the Sexes." During the 1970s, women were fighting for equal rights. Many people were calling for improvements to the Equal Pay Act of 1963. This law said that men and women should make the same **wages** for the same work. Despite the law, women continued to receive less pay, and they were still **discriminated** against. Public pressure is often needed to see laws fully enforced. During the 1970s, the pressure was strong. **Activists** continued to fight. The Equal Pay Act of 1963 led to the Equal Rights Amendment (ERA) of 1972.

The ERA stated that equal rights should be given to all people, regardless of sex. The United States Senate passed the law to make it part of the U.S. Constitution. The decision then went to the states. Despite high levels of activism and the ensuing popular support, the states did not **ratify** the act into law. The ERA would have been another major step forward in the fight for equality, after women won the right to vote in 1920.

Equal Prize Money

Soccer, basketball, and golf continue to have enormous pay **disparities**, *while tennis prize money is equal. This wasn't the case until Billie Jean King threatened to* **boycott** *the U.S. Open in 1973 unless women and men earned equally. Only a year before, in 1972, King made $10,000 in prize money compared to the men's winner, Ilie Năstase, who made $25,000. The French Open was the last tournament to not award equal prize money for both men and women—in 2006.*

Two Players

Bobby Riggs was one of the best male tennis players of all time. At one point, he was the number-one ranked player. He had six major titles. He didn't think women could play tennis as well as men, and he wanted to prove it. In 1973, at the age of 55, Riggs asked Billie Jean King to play him, but she turned him down. Instead, on Mother's Day in 1973, Riggs played Margaret Court. Court was 30 years old at the time of Riggs's challenge and the number-one ranked player in the world. Riggs used **drop shots** when Court stood closer to the **baseline**, and Court couldn't track them down in time. Riggs also lobbed the ball over Court's head, where she couldn't return the ball. Riggs defeated Court in straight sets, 6–2 and 6–1. His win put him on the cover of *Sports Illustrated* and *Time* magazines.

During Margaret Court's career, she won 24 Grand Slam singles and 21 Grand Slam mixed doubles.

Using his popularity as a lure, Riggs once again challenged King to a match. He offered $100,000 in prize money to whichever player won. Riggs offered the money because he was a gambler and wasn't worried about defeating King. After his easy defeat over Court, Riggs spent most of his time taunting and degrading female tennis players. King thought it was more important than ever to show everyone in the world that women could play as well as men. King, one of the best female tennis players of all time, accepted his challenge.

Billie Jean King stands on the court during a match at Wimbledon in England.

In 1973, she was 29 years old. In her prime, King had already won 10 singles championships. King thought that women were equal to men and that they could play just as well. She wanted to play Riggs because she wanted to prove that he was wrong about women playing an **inferior** tennis game. She also hoped to inspire girls to play any sport they wanted, without feeling like they weren't good enough to play. King helped bring the ERA into the spotlight. She wanted Americans to unite and to see women as just as capable as men. In doing so, men and women could cooperate and focus on bigger issues, such as **humanitarianism** and **minority** rights. When Riggs offered the winner the same prize money, King acted on the opportunity to prove that women could earn and deserve the same wages and rewards as men.

The Original 9

The "Original 9" group of female tennis players thought it was unfair that women played for less money than men. They spoke with Jack Kramer, a chairman of the Pacific Southwest Championships, to offer equal pay for the tournament, but he refused. The Original 9 were furious, boycotted the tournament, and formed the independent Virginia Slims **Circuit***. This circuit became the Women's Tennis Association (WTA). Many female players are part of this league today.*

CHAPTER 3

The Battle of the Sexes

This match was more important than any other tennis match that had ever been played. At least, it was for Billie Jean King. She had to show the entire world that women could play as well as men. Also nerve-racking were the almost 30,500 spectators packed into the Houston, Texas, Astrodome. She and Riggs had expected to play in front of a couple hundred people at most. King felt the pressure of playing in a televised match, which was featured on primetime television. More than 50 million Americans watched the game, and 90 million viewers watched worldwide, wanting to see if history would be made. Celebrities attended the match, including sports journalist Howard Cosell and boxer George Foreman, who also served, comically, as King's bodyguard.

Though King and Riggs did not know each other before the match, after the match they became lifelong friends.

Understandably, King didn't want to make any mistakes. She played very carefully. She hit long shots towards Riggs's baseline. She didn't try anything fancy. She wasn't playing to look pretty. She was playing to win.

Riggs, on the other hand, played with wild **abandon**. He thought defeating King would be easy. Although King played hard, Riggs broke her serve in the first set. This means that Riggs won a game that King was serving, which put him ahead in games.

King's athleticism could not be matched by Riggs.

King feared that if she lost the first set, then no one would believe she could come back from behind. She later said, "I thought it would set us back 50 years if I didn't win that match. It would ruin the women's tour and affect all women's self esteem." It's easy to see how much she felt she needed to win!

King was tired, worried, and losing. But she refused to give up. She had run Riggs around so much that he was getting tired. King tied the score and kept playing hard. She didn't want to ruin all the hard work she had just done. King won the first set.

Though Riggs was very confident entering the match, he struggled to score during actual play.

King kept her energy going to win the second set 6–3. After the pressure of the rest of the match, King felt both relief and anxiety to play the final set. Once again, Riggs won three games to King's six. Suddenly, it was match point. If King won this point, then she would win the whole match. And she did! The crowd cheered, and King couldn't believe her eyes. She had defeated a man and had shown the world that women were just as good as men at sports.

The Threat of a Boycott

Billie Jean King had a fair amount of influence leading up to the match. Jack Kramer was a former tennis player and the chairman of the Pacific Southwest Championships. He wanted to announce the Battle of the Sexes. King was upset because he wouldn't change the rules to let women earn the same amount of money as men. King said that she would not play if Kramer announced the event. The American Broadcasting Company (ABC) chose Howard Cosell to announce the match.

The Time is NOW

The 1960s were a time of great change. The **Civil Rights** Movement had inspired many other minorities to fight for their rights. One group fought for women's rights and is still around today. It's called the National Organization for Women (NOW). The group was formed on June 30, 1966. The group wanted to protect women and to help women find their voices.

NOW fights for laws to give women equal rights as men. NOW wants to help women make the same pay as men. The group hopes to teach others about how **racism** is wrong, and it helps **LGBT** people fight for equal rights.

CHAPTER 4

The Hero

When Bobby Riggs hit a backhand volley into the net on match point, Billie Jean King threw her racquet into the air. She knew she had changed the world. King had taken the first step in changing how men saw women in sports. She had also changed how women and girls saw themselves. Two weeks after her win, King said she learned that the women at a Philadelphia newspaper "had stormed into their bosses' offices and demanded raises on the spot." King knew that all of her practicing and hard work had been well worth it.

After the match, King said that girls came down from the stands to thank her for playing and for winning. The champion also said that "fathers came up with tears in their eyes. And many

Riggs knew that King had been the better player and after the match he showed good sportsmanship.

of their daughters started playing tennis." King's defeat of a man showed little girls that they didn't have to be afraid to shine. And her victory showed boys that it was good to accept girls, because the girls were just as good as the boys.

In response to a reporter who asked what impact her win had on women's tennis, King replied, "It's funny how when a woman does something, they always think we only affect half of the population." King reported that the following year, the women's and men's professional tours marked the highest spectator

King lifts her trophy up so the crowd can see it after beating Riggs.

attendance of any previous year. In addition, the number of girls attending tennis camps and other sports camps skyrocketed after the Battle of the Sexes.

In 1971, King became the first woman to earn more than $100,000 for prizes in a single season. She made $117,000. King won $100,000 just for winning the Battle of the Sexes. She accepted her check from none other than George Foreman, one of the first superstar athletes in the United States. The following year, she made almost 10 times the amount of money she earned in 1971!

The win meant a lot to King as a professional, but it also meant a lot to women athletes everywhere.

For his part, Riggs walked up to the net and said, "I underestimated you." He was embarrassed by his loss. He was so upset that he returned to his hotel and wouldn't come out for four hours! Riggs said that King was able to return all of his serves and that he couldn't lob the ball over her head. Riggs admitted that he had spent too much time hyping the match instead of training for it.

Big Business

While King was a star player before the match, her Battle of the Sexes triumph launched her into immediate popularity. Big companies saw King's win as an opportunity for advertising. Advertisers flocked to her side, ready to sign contracts and talk business. King accepted numerous **endorsements***, and advertised for Colgate toothpaste, Adidas sneakers, Wimbledon racquets, and Sunbeam hair curlers. The following year, King's income reportedly neared $1 million.*

Perfection in Adaptation

Billie Jean King's usual style of play was one where she would serve the ball and then run up to the net. She was good at volleys. She watched Margaret Court play Bobby Riggs and saw that he lobbed the ball over Court's head. Court lost many points because she was unable to get to the ball. King learned that she could not run up to the net when she played Riggs because it wouldn't work.

She forced Riggs to play from the baseline. King ran him back and forth across the court for the entire match. He was weary and his shots were weak. Sometimes he missed a shot. Other times, he couldn't get to the ball. Riggs never adjusted to the new style, and he lost the match.

CHAPTER 5

Equality in Sports

Before Billie Jean King's victory, she was fighting for women's rights. She was part of the Original 9, a group of nine women who kicked **feminism** into high gear. In 1970, women's tennis players prepared to play at the Pacific Southwest Championships. Organizers of the tournament offered to pay the men eight times as much as the women. Unhappy with the wage gap, the nine women spoke with Gladys Heldman, a tennis publisher. They joined forces with Joseph Cullman, the chairman of Phillip Morris, a cigarette manufacturer.

On September 23, 1970, the women joined the Virginia Slims Circuit, named after a type of cigarette. They signed contracts for $1, and in 1971 played a series of 19 tournaments in the new circuit. The Original 9 drew attention to the wage discrimination

In 2013, Billie Jean King spoke during the 34th annual Salute to Women in Sports Awards in New York City.

between men's and women's tennis. The Virginia Slims Circuit became the Women's Tennis Association, which organizes scores, rankings, and other information about women's tennis players and still exists today.

In 1973, two years after the game where King beat Riggs, King became the first president of the WTA. King formed the Women's Sports Foundation in 1974. The foundation states that it is "dedicated to creating leaders by ensuring all girls access to sports." The foundation provides support for female athletes, including scholarships, grants for traveling to sporting events,

The winner of the WTA Finals is awarded the Billie Jean King Trophy.

and access to equipment. The foundation also published a magazine, originally titled *womenSports*. The magazine was dedicated to female athletes and their accomplishments. The magazine changed titles several times over the years, but was one of the first magazines to showcase female athletes' accomplishments and deeds.

In the 1970s, King cofounded World TeamTennis, which, according to her, "[is my] philosophy of life in action—men and women, competing together, on a team, and both genders making equal contributions to the result." Most famous tennis players have played for the Billie Jean King Trophy, named after its founder. King felt that she was born to help women feel equal to men. She did this in many ways. When she beat Bobby Riggs, she helped girls find their voice. Many girls joined tennis and went to camps after she won. Using her motto of "equal opportunity for boys and girls," she told girls that they could be whatever they wanted to be and that they were strong. She also told boys that they could enjoy playing tennis with girls and that they were still strong. They didn't need to be afraid of the girls, and they could still play hard.

Equality Under the Law

Title IX is a law that says a person can't be treated unfairly because of their sex. It's meant for schools, but it is used in general as well. Billie Jean King told the U.S. Congress that Title IX was really important for women. She thought that it would help women get into good colleges. King thought that getting women into the same good schools men went to would help them get good jobs as well.

1966
King wins her first major singles championship at Wimbledon.

1939
Riggs is ranked first in the world for tennis.

1930

1960

1967
King becomes the top-ranked women's tennis player.

1972

King wins the U.S. Open, French Open, and Wimbledon, claiming three Grand Slam titles in one year.

1970

1973

Riggs defeats Margaret Court in the "Mother's Day Massacre."

1973

King defeats Riggs in the "Battle of the Sexes."

Billie Jean King said she played Bobby Riggs as much for women's rights as for prize money. How do you think she felt after winning the match? Why does it matter that King won the Battle of the Sexes?

Look at the spectators in this picture. Are they mostly men or women? Do they look happy for Billie Jean King?

In this picture, Billie Jean King is holding up a large trophy. How was this moment important for both men and women watching the match?

Learn More

BOOKS

Gitlin, Martin. *Powerful Moments in Sports: The Most Significant Sporting Events in American History.* Lanham, MD: Rowman and Littlefield, 2017.

Stabler, David. *Kid Athletes: True Tales of Childhood from Sports Legends.* Kid Legends. Philadelphia: Quirk Books, 2015.

Wendorff, Anne. *Tennis.* Minneapolis: Bellwether Media, 2010.

ON THE WEB

Billie Jean King's Official Website
https://www.billiejeanking.com

History's Battle of the Sexes
http://www.history.com/this-day-in-history/king-triumphs-in-battle-of-sexes

Women's Tennis Association
http://www.wtatennis.com

GLOSSARY

abandon (uh-BAN-din) a feeling of freedom, without caution or care

activists (AK-tuh-vists) people who fight for a cause or belief

baseline (BEYS-lahyn) the boundary line at either end of a tennis court

boycott (BOI-kaht) to refuse to buy goods or support certain businesses due to one's beliefs or ideals

circuit (SUR-kit) a league

civil rights (SIH-vul RAHYTS) the rights that every person should have regardless of his or her sex, race, or religion

discriminated (dih-SKRIH-mih-nay-tid) treated differently regardless of skill or worth

disparities (dih-SPER-ih-teez) differences or inequalities

drop shots (DRAHP SHAHTS) delicately hit shots that drop quickly after crossing the net

endorsements (in-DORS-mints) money earned from advertising for products

feminism (FEH-mih-nih-zum) the belief that women should have the same rights as men

humanitarianism (hyuu-man-ih-TER-ee-uh-nih-zum) the belief that human beings should be concerned about each other's health and wellbeing

inferior (in-FEER-ee-ur) having little value

LGBT (ELL-JEE-BEE-TEE) an abbreviation for lesbian, gay, bisexual, and transgender

minority (mai-NOR-ih-tee) a group that is less powerful regardless of the number of people in the group

racism (RAY-sih-zum) hatred or intolerance of another race or other races

ratify (RAT-ih-fai) to formally approve

wages (WAY-jihz) a salary

INDEX